Domestic Karma

poems by

Andrea Carter Brown

Finishing Line Press
Georgetown, Kentucky

Domestic Karma

Copyright © 2018 by Andrea Carter Brown
ISBN 978-1-63534-731-9 First Edition
All rights reserved under International and Pan-American Copyright Conventions. No part of this book may be reproduced in any manner whatsoever without written permission from the publisher, except in the case of brief quotations embodied in critical articles and reviews.

ACKNOWLEDGMENTS

Grateful acknowledgment is made to the editors of the following journals and anthologies in which some of these poems, or earlier versions of them, previously appeared:

Askew Poetry Journal: "The Man Who Loves Apples" and "Urban Encounter in Time of Drought"
Atlanta Review: "Domestic Karma" (print)
BigCityLit: "Domestic Karma" (online)
Birmingham Poetry Review: "*Salade niçoise*, In Memoriam"
Crab Orchard Review: "Getting Out the Vote"
The Denny Poems: "After a Sleepless Night I Cook"
Five Points: "In the Desert"
The Gettysburg Review: "*Die goldene Zeit*"
Like Light: "To a Midge"
The Marlboro Review: "Full"
Miramar: "Aubade with Spider and Flag" and "The Morning After"
Ploughshares: "Blues, For Bill"

Publisher: Leah Maines
Editor: Christen Kincaid
Cover Art: © Linda Slocum, "Early Bird", 2017, Photography, 2432 x 4320 pixels, Courtesy of the artist. www.worksbyhand.com
Author Photo: © Lauren Del Santoro França 2018

Printed in the USA on acid-free paper.
Order online: www.finishinglinepress.com
also available on amazon.com

Author inquiries and mail orders:
Finishing Line Press
P. O. Box 1626
Georgetown, Kentucky 40324
U. S. A.

Table of Contents

Aubade with Spider and Flag 1

Blues, For Bill 2

Full 3

The SECOND Anniversary 5

August 6th 6

Later, Venus 11

The Man Who Loves Apples 12

After a Sleepless Night I Cook 13

Urban Encounter in Time of Drought 14

Domestic Karma 15

Die goldene Zeit 16

The Lord's Prayer 17

Getting Out the Vote 18

Another Anniversary 21

September Song 22

O, Chanticleer 23

The Morning After 25

Salade niçoise, In Memoriam 26

In the Desert 27

The Folding Cliffs 28

To a Midge 31

Notes 32

To the memory of my parents
Evelyn M. Brown and Andrew W. Brown
and
For T. S. D., in medias res
as always

Aubade with Spider and Flag

How do the spiders know it's safe
to spin their webs? That the parched
winds funneling through the canyons

will not rip them from their moorings,
a late spring rain illuminate their work
for all to see? After a spattering too slight

to call a shower, I fetch the papers. Since
yesterday, a gossamer scrim has straddled
the driveway, as high as the parapet

of the house, so low I can barely duck
under it. And there, smack in the middle,
a black spider big as my thumb waits

for something edible to be caught, unable
to escape. Lately I've regretted not burying
Dad with the other veterans as he wished.

Why did I insist on sticking him with
his parents, sister, and grandparents
in the family plot above Cemetery Curve

in the town he fought a war to leave?
Later today, I'll look for the little flag
with forty-eight stars he used to carry

in parades, hoping the moths haven't
eaten holes in it, to hang outside
the front gate come this Memorial Day.

Blues, For Bill

How fitting that he should come back as blues,
the whole panoply from indigo to ultramarine
on two wings, as cows lumbered up the swale

to a hilltop pasture, the sun sunk behind the now
truly named Blue Ridge, the world in deepening
shadow. How perfect that he should come back

as a butterfly, and yet, given his love of words
and where they come from, how apt it should be
in the blues of a Red-spotted Purple, southerly

conspecific to the White Admiral she might find
in the city where they lived. This is her first summer
in this state; this is the first blue butterfly she's

ever seen. She is wearing blue jeans. She stands
just beyond the shade of a stately Chinese elm,
watching day fade. Except for the cattle, it is

utterly quiet. The butterfly alights on her right hip
and stays, its quivering subsiding slowly to calm.
She could touch it, but doesn't. The Incas believed

warriors fallen in battle visit loved ones left behind
as butterflies, she learns later. She knows very little
of this then. She still doesn't know what happened

to his ashes, his cookbooks and jazz, the last message
she left. She knows where his books went, who took
in Velcro. To satisfy him she learned the difference

between twilight and dusk. She tries not to budge,
to breathe as lightly as she can. With nightfall, he lifts
off. She knows how lucky she is. How lucky she was.

Full

i

The moon is fat and orange and round.
It pops up above the clouds in the angle
between telephone wires and flag pole.
In the blue spruces across the pond, two
great horned owls hoot as they swoop,
screech when perched. Their beaks open
and close a second before the cry carries
to this side of the valley. From time
to time, their heads swivel full circle,
amber saucer eyes taking everything in.

ii

The moon is plump and pink and friendly.
In the pause between the rhythmic jostling
of cobbles by ocean: clicking. A flashlight
finds a porcupine in the apple tree, eating,
teeth grooves in the white flesh between claws.
Light shining in the red eyes doesn't interrupt
his concentration. He looks in this direction
then resumes the methodical consumption
of every ripe apple within reach, moving
along the branch until hidden by leaves.

iii

The moon is hiding behind the house. Some
stars come out. In the yellow bedroom, under
a blue comforter, the sleeper searches the river
valley she knows by heart. Deep snow covers

the land; the roads are closed. In a round tower
living room ringed by windows, the aunt
who died a month ago is waiting to give her
tea and chocolates. In her leafy tree house
high in the sugar maples, the aunt waits.

THE SECOND ANNIVERSARY

the first sign says, held
high on a stick by a man
who makes eye contact

as I stop for a red light.
It's pouring. The next sign
is covered by a black plastic

garbage bag—not to keep it
dry, I realize. More like a small
body bag, seeing the next, and

the next. Dozens of protesters
line the arms of the intersection
where Arrow Highway crosses

Indian Hill Boulevard. They
silently hold up placards: *1500
Dead Soldiers* alternates with *War*

Creates Widows and Orphans.
All day long I've been thinking
about widows and orphans,

editing an article about the poem
I heard, as if I had no Ear drafted
by Dickinson during the Civil War.

It's a new job, my first since
we moved across the continent
to get away from Ground Zero.

House finches, golden here gorging
on the orange fruits of the purple
passion flower, fall silent, waiting

out the downpour. Through the torrent
that streams down the windshield
I cannot see red turn green.

August 6th

Tomorrow.
Dad would have been 105.
Beach supposed to be cloudy.
Tide too high to walk easily.
Later, in his memory,
shall I eat his favorite
oysters or ice cream?

*

After his 100th, it became more
difficult to imagine him.

*

The genes in my family run to
early nineties. Will I
make it that far?

*

Seventy years ago today the bomb
was dropped on Hiroshima. Still
in uniform, sent to Biarritz
after victory in the European
Theater of Operations, Dad
no doubt rejoiced at the news.
He could come home soon.
Did he want to?

*

Another bomb two days later
to seal the deal.

*

Fat Man.
Baker.
Sugar.
Checkmate.
Zucchini.
Moth.
Trinity.
Diablo.
Climax.

Names.

How long would it be
before we began to understand
the damage done?

*

A six hour drive north of here,
on the rain shadow side
of the mountains, a wind-blasted
wasteland, parched
even before this current
four-year drought, the remains
of a camp where American citizens
of Japanese descent were interned
during the war, their loyalties
suspect.

*

A young boy during World War I,
ashamed his parents and grandparents
still spoke German at home,
Dad came to hate all things
German, including

the last name he
persisted in misattributing
to a non-existent Scottish ancestor
as long as he lived.

*

Allowed to bring
a single small suitcase
they crafted bowls
to perform tea ceremonies,
brushed ink on paper scrolls
for the alcoves of flimsy shacks
which were either
beastly hot or freezing cold.

*

In the muddy camps just north
of the Pyrenees used
previously to intern refugees
of the Spanish Civil War,
transported Jews made
a purse woven out of weeds,
a wedding invitation
bride and groom on either side
of a menorah,
a child's white party dress
with a yellow star appliquéd
above her heart, the word
Juif embroidered in black
across the center.

*

A WWII soldier
refused to talk about the war
although he crossed
the Rhine
on a pontoon bridge
with Patton.
The soldier's daughter
visits the camp
hidden above the town
Goethe, Schiller, and Liszt
called home.

*

Russian soldiers stationed
near Weimar
visit the camp on leave.
A just-married couple,
he in brown Soviet dress uniform,
she in a frilly white gown and veil,
clutching three red chrysanthemums,
pose outside the main gate
as a friend photographs them.

JEDEM DAS SEINE

To each his own

backwards
above the grinning
newlyweds.

*

In June, our neighbor Abe
finally died. Before he lost

his mind, he enjoyed telling
and retelling the story
of how many camps
he survived, how he met
his wife in one of them,
how they came to this country, tried
chicken farming in New Jersey
before he made it good
here in Los Angeles,
first as deli counter man,
later making pink
cardboard boxes
for rugelach and Danish.

*

Cooking dinner, I look
at his empty home,
a *For Sale* sign in the front yard.
Nights when I can't sleep,
I miss the lights
constantly on
in his bedroom window.

*

Dad never got to see
our home out here.
Tomorrow, in his honor,
I'll walk the fog-shrouded beach,
high-tide steep,
then celebrate with
oysters, strawberries,
and ice cream.

Later, Venus

Day of jackhammer, then sledge-
    hammer. Explosive kerplunk,
        concrete chunks into dumpster

Day of chainsaw, eucalyptus trunks
    reduced to lengths one man can hoist
        into the chipper, intermittent moan

Day of milky overflow of laundry water,
    gray, clotted with clumps, pooling on brick
        around pear tree, paired silver maples

Bark darkens, the slender exposed seam
    of clay unable to absorb any more,
        refusing, fed up. The foul pond

Bite of chipper again after lunch break, dome
    of rubber tree reduced, its full leafy moon
        wanes by quarter to new, to blue

Winds gust as the front moves through, drops
    palm fronds to the ground, heavy as bodies,
        razor sharp, splatter of released fruits

Twigs, branches, leaves litter the lawn. I give
    up raking. Later, Venus, a dark speck,
        will pass between us and the sun

The Man Who Loves Apples

I married a man who loves apples, who could eat
several a day, and sometimes does. Who prefers
the flesh juicy, crisp, tart but not too, who every fall

bemoans the Galas and Fujis found on the West Coast:
cloyingly sweet, soft, soon mushy, without that crunch
he craves. Delicious he won't touch; Granny Smiths,

sour, tough of skin, the choice of desperation. Pink
Ladies, if they are small and recently picked, he will
eat, but not enthusiastically. Years after we moved

to LA, I thought he would never reconcile himself
to life without Macs, Macouns, and best of all, his
favorite hard to find Winesaps, especially Staymans,

their season short and iffy. Persnickety to grow,
beloved of worms, not easily shipped, they've fallen
out of favor. My husband speaks so highly of them

our farmers market avocado guru put in a few trees
and saves the entire harvest for Tom, paltry though
it is. He hasn't the heart to tell Frank they don't taste

right. No cold snap early, long, or deep enough to set
the flavor. Still Tom buys them, lets Frank continue
to believe he's doing a good thing. Which he is.

After a Sleepless Night I Cook

The day we saw the shrike we play *Shanghai*
until midnight when, bleary-eyed from trying
to match tiles so the pyramid will collapse

and the green dragon breathe red fire
on your computer screen, we turn
in and still I can't sleep for thorns

on which mice are impaled and wrens
crying as they dry in the sun. Then the owl
starts to squawk from his favorite dead branch

above the parking lot, after which an ambulance
barrels down Barham, the pattern of its
high-pitched siren signaling which life-

saving equipment will be needed, setting
off the coyotes which in turn triggers
another damn owl who contributes his hoots

to the chorus. I want to scream. When
the racket reaches its peak, the soft
gurgle of your breathing breaks into

a snore. Dawn bleeds through the drapes
before I nod off. That night I try
Joe Montana's recipe for veal piccata

buried inside the *Enquirer* bought because
Little Joe was dying. For two, it calls for three
heaping tablespoons of capers and a whole

lemon peeled and chopped. Pulling back
pith with a paring knife, the juice
stings the slits in my dry fingers but,

married to the briny buds picked by hand
from the shrub with spines and reduced,
the sour lost its bite and was good.

Urban Encounter in Time of Drought

A black snake about two feet long, slender
as a pencil, suns itself on a quiet side street.

It doesn't budge as I approach. Is it dead?
The merest nudge with a stick, it sidewinds

into the shrubbery. Terrified as I have been
of snakes ever since our Brownie troop visited

the herpetologist who released her specimens
and let them crawl freely around the room,

I am sorry to chase this one away. After all,
how often does one see a snake in Hollywood?

It hardly rained all winter. Water restrictions
in effect, rationing is next. Wild animals

come down from the tinder-dry hills.
As long as we can, we'll water the yard,

run the fountain, and fill the birdbath.
Let the animals come. Even the snakes.

Domestic Karma

Pair of pulleys, a circle of rope
stretched taut into parallel lines

dividing the driveway, lime tree
from lemon and tangerine. Small

square wicker basket, wooden
clothes pins. The week's worth

of suspended shirts tickles aloe,
hens and chicks. Pillowcases,

damp sheets release memories
of rumpled sleep and bad dreams

to the breeze. Clean underwear
made fresh for the body you love

to undress; socks newly plumped
cushion steps. Monday morning

again. May this ritual help us get
through the week between tests

and results. May it bring six
months of Mondays like this,

shirts loving sun on shoulders,
fear faded as favorite blue jeans

pinned to the line, socks ready
to take us wherever we want.

Die goldene Zeit
after an anonymous print

You don't need to know German to get
the picture. A quartet of ladies, mantles
draped over diaphanous gowns, laurel
leaves braided into their hair, lounge

in a boat rowed with a single lute-shaped
oar. One plays a lyre, a second the harp.
The rest listen to a singer, score in hand.
A child, leaning over the prow, dangles

garlands of roses in the water. The women
wear white, green, or blue. The men, in gray,
black, and brown echo the hull, the bay,
and temple-strewn shore. One imagines

deep conversation, though this troupe conveys
a funereal air, as though art—for what else
is *The Golden Age?*—looks like a grown-up

version of Wynken, Blynken, and Nod, their
skiff set out from god knows where; without
sail or stars, the group adrift, their port unclear.

The Lord's Prayer

At Disney Hall, the Welsh baritone famous
for playing Wagnerian heroes ends his encore
with *The Lord's Prayer*. Seeing me scowl,
my musician husband whispers *Can't you*

get past the words to the beauty of his voice?
But he doesn't hear my aunt practicing it
for weddings and funerals, those Sundays
I stood next to Mother as she belted it out.

I must have sung it dozens of times myself
when I still believed. The hours we spent
discussing the virtues of different recordings:
her favorite, Marian Anderson's. We debated

which words to emphasize, which syllables,
and why; the merits of *trespasses* versus *debts*,
which art or *who*. When I wake the morning
after the concert, I cannot get the words out

of my mind—*Our Father*, as I brew coffee;
Hallowed be, in the shower; *Give us*, making
the bed; *Forgive us*, as I fight with my husband
over who should order Thanksgiving flowers

for his parents; *as we forgive*, reviewing yet
another incorrect bill from the City of Hope;
and *Lead us*, as I sit down to write these lines.
For as much as I no longer believe *Thine is*

the power, the glory, here I am, hijacked by
the past. This coming Wednesday is the fifth
anniversary of her death. In this way I keep
faith with my mother. *For ever and ever. Amen.*

Getting Out the Vote
after Rogier van der Weyden

A hard-worn garden complex in Las Vegas.
Last stop of a long, desiccating day. Dented
door, much painted. Through it, children's
laughter, muted: at least someone is home.

Four raps on the brass knocker. A friendly
Latino woman opens the door, surprised
to find two middle-aged Anglo women.
"Grassroots volunteers for the campaign,"

they introduce themselves, "We're looking
for," one consults a clipboard, "Luis Gonzalez."
According to the printout, he is the only
voter living here. "Is he home?" "Yes."

Pause. "Can we speak with him?" "You'll
have to come inside." Longer pause. "We're
not supposed to." "He's paralyzed." The two
volunteers exchange glances, decide to break

the rules. Smiling, she leads them down a hall
into a small bedroom. In the far corner, a man
lies on a single bed. He is wearing nothing but
a T-shirt and disposable underpants. In his eyes,

a wild expression which subsides only after
the young woman, his daughter it turns out,
explains who these strangers are. Speaking
for him, she tells them: Yes, he wants to vote.

No, he isn't registered. This will be his first
election since becoming a citizen, since
being paralyzed. Thus, the Q & A begins,
the patient daughter switching easily

between English and Spanish, as together
they complete the complicated form. *Citizen*:
Yes. *Over 18*: Yes. *Name: Last, First, Middle*.
But he has two last names; they make one

the middle. *Address*: easy. *Date of birth*:
the shocker. How young he is, given
how old he looks. *Place of birth*: Veracruz,
Mexico. *Driver's License*: No. *State Photo*

ID: to both volunteers' relief, he has one.
The daughter rattles off the number she
knows by heart. *Signature*: their hearts
sink, assuming he can't write. Instead,

the daughter squeezes into the space
between the wall and the bed, holds
the clipboard steady, helps him get
a firm grip on the pen, and guides

his hand to the slender rectangle
within which he must sign. And he
does, in cramped, shaky script, legible
to the Anglos, who are satisfied it will

pass muster. This is one registration
they want to get right. May every clerk
who lays eyes on it send it on its way
without a hitch. May his absentee ballot

arrive. In time. *En español*. May this
man, who has waited so long to vote,
whose life has been unspeakably hard,
be able to cast his first vote for a President

of the "Party of the Poor," as his daughter
enthusiastically volunteers. Five people
in that small square room. At the center,
a wasted man. On his left, his wife

gently strokes his forearm with one finger;
on his right, his daughter with children
of her own fills in the date. At the foot
of the bed, two Anglo women look on

reverently, like donors consigned to
a side panel or corner of the altarpiece.
Humbled, they try not to stare. Instead,
unaware until they confess it later to

each other, they look at his feet. The nails,
especially. So clean, and trimmed. Buffed
even. The care that went into that. They
take in the room's cleanliness, the lack

of smell, the absence of medical equipment,
the second bed for the wife, the man's bed
positioned so he can see out the window.
Struggling not to lose it, the Anglo women

summon up "Adíos"—to the man, his daughter,
and the wife, who responds, "Ve con Dios,"
using the familiar form of the verb. Giggles,
suddenly: unsuspected by the grown-ups,

three of the daughter's children are hiding
under the bed. Having heard and understood
every word, Spanish and English, in unison
they chime in "Good-bye," a knowing

look in their eyes. Long after the two
volunteers hurry back to the County
Clerk to deliver this voter registration
before the deadline, both women

will worry about him, will be haunted
by the look in his eyes, his wasted legs
and dainty feet, will hope this vote
brings Luis Martín-González peace.

Another Anniversary
after William Carlos Williams

On the eve of another anniversary I am stuck
in traffic. Miracle Mile Engine No. 1 is blocking

the intersection. The truck is polished to perfection,
its crimson ruby rich, the chrome shining so brightly,

it hurts my eyes to look. Inside, the crew stares
out the windows, relaxed, their pressed uniforms

still neat, unwrinkled. False alarm or lunch break,
no one seems in a hurry. As the cab creeps forward,

9-11-01 in small gilt numbers inches past. Was this
one of the trucks, are they some of the firefighters

who poured into our wounded neighborhood
to pitch in when so much had been destroyed,

so many lost? In my new home, a continent from
that blighted life, I salute them. For remembering.

September Song
September 11, 2014

All day long the wren sings to me.
I exaggerate. All day long the wren
sings: repeated extended dry trills
with a slight pause between each.

To attract a mate? Unlikely, it being
fall. To stake a claim to this clear view
of bird bath or fountain? Out of sheer
pleasure would be my guess, the day

fresh, sunny, warm but not hot,
the accumulated dust of summer
washed away by the first real rain
in months, the air clean enough

to breathe easily again. He moves.
A branch or two higher in the dying tree,
more beloved of birds with its bounty
of decay. I hear him as if he perched

in my hand, but hidden he stays.
A flash, a shadow, a leaf stirs,
his insistent song sufficient to bring
comfort, to redeem our shared day.

O, Chanticleer

I

O, Chanticleer, who twirls in the wind
above clock towers, the national symbol
not a bird of prey but a domestic fowl,
the source of eggs that make delicious

omelettes aux fines herbes. O, Louis XVI,
with your wife whose wigs hosted birds,
in sending Lafayette to help a colonial
revolt destroy a hated rival, could you

not see ahead how *Liberté, Égalité,
Fraternité* would come home to roost
and cost you your head, the Ancien Régime
guillotined out of existence by the Terror?

Shoulder to shoulder we stand with our first
allies, the President promises, echoing other
heads of state. But hindsight, foresight, what
to do against fanatics who would turn back

the clock, not a couple hundred years, but
thousands—the punishment for a woman
talking to a man outside her family, the loss
of her head, for a "blasphemer," his tongue.

A survivor of *le onze neuf* as 9/11 is known
in France, writes these lines the morning
after November 13th. *Le treize onze* as this
day will no doubt become known, no other

information needed. In solidarity I put on
a royal blue shirt, tie a white and red bandana
jauntily around my throat, and make myself
go out to sign yet another condolence book.

II

O, *Tricolore*, with your blue, white, and red
flapping at half-mast above masses of flowers,
photos, stuffed animals, candles drowning
in puddles of wax, on signs we promise

never to forget, *Nous n'oublierons jamais.* O,
somber decorated police officer in body armor,
handgun at his waist, who pats down each visitor
thoroughly before allowing each to pass through

a bulletproof plexiglass box with two locked doors.
O, elegantly-dressed woman who silently ushers
each of us in turn to the dimmed conference room
and leaves us alone, closing the door. O, fragrant

white roses and hydrangea beside the open book.
How could you not realize the message would need
to be *en français?* Trying not to make mistakes,
your sympathy joins that of mayors, ambassadors,

chefs, secretaries, young and old, European,
American—you can tell from our handwriting—
all of us united in the desire, the need to express
our love against hopelessness, anger, and grief.

The Morning After
December 3, 2015

From my kitchen window I watch the wind
toss the giant birds of paradise, tear citrus,
silver maple, and pear leaves from the trees,

blow over a potted palm too heavy to budge.
Yesterday I woke up remembering Mother
died ten years ago this morning; I planted

these trees in her memory. The ground
is littered with dead branches, the heavy
desiccated fronds with needle sharp teeth.

This is the desert doing its fall cleaning,
washing away the grit of another long hot
dry summer, the months without rain.

The mountains are visible again, crest line
crisp. Last night, a crescent moon precise
as a sharpened scimitar hung above our house,

the completion of its circle seeming to smile.
Later Orion, the stars of his sword and shield
visible, straddled the velvet dark sky, keeping

guard over us. The morning after the attack
in San Bernardino, I stare out my window.
The wind tosses the trees this way and that.

Salade niçoise, In Memoriam
Whitmanesque

I celebrate the dark tuna, packed in olive oil.
The *pommes de terre*, apples of the earth, sliced,

barely cooked, then gently tossed with stock,
vinegar, more olive oil, scallions, chopped

parsley to finish. I sing of July's tomatoes,
bursting with flavor, vivid red; crunchy green

peppers just arrived at the farmers market,
ringed; blanched string beans, chilled. I thank

our neighbor's chickens, whose blue eggs,
hard-boiled, peel easily and quarter neatly.

Liberally strew the tiny local black olives,
capers (my invention). Arrange artfully

on a bed of Little Gems; lay on anchovies
like the spokes of a wheel. All morning

the day after Bastille Day, I make this
from scratch for you, city never visited,

sun-drenched Nice, in grief, with love,
because I do not know what else to do.

In the Desert

You didn't get to see the scrub jay's sky
blue pinstriped bib, the deep purple
flash of the black-chinned hummingbird.

You'll never see a black-throated sparrow's
nest woven into the yucca's slender spines
like a ball of tumbleweed come to rest.

You won't ever hear, then see, the ladder-
backed woodpecker perched at the very top
of a Joshua Tree drill last spring's seed pods

with his beak. You didn't live to write
your desert poem telling me why someone
named that cactus after a hero in the Bible.

For you, who peppered your poems with
the language of your faith, I'll use *yarmulke*
to describe the woodpecker's crimson cap.

The Folding Cliffs
after W. S. Merwin

Neither of us noticed the gradual shift
    from rosy to yellow, the sinking
        cheeks. We blamed

sodden pillows and sheets on bad
    dreams, out of control blood
        sugar. Looking

at the photo of us perched halfway up
    the cliffs, dripping with sweat
        but aglow with a sense

of accomplishment, the ravage can't
    be hidden by high spirits.
        It was our first time

on the islands, a big anniversary trip.
    Evenings on the lanai watching
        dramatic sunsets, we read

out loud to each other, taking turns,
    the poet's epic retelling of how
        disease was used to wrest

this land from the native Hawaiians
    who had themselves emigrated
        in outrigger canoes

across the ocean to this archipelago
    rising from below. We came
        to bird, but the birds

were few and hard to see: endemic species
    almost wiped out by mosquitoes
        inadvertently introduced.

The native birds survive in the sunken
 caldera of extinct volcanoes
  above the mosquito line—

a bright scarlet *'i'iwi* with a sickle bill
 deep in the lush collapsed cone
  behind the Folding Cliffs—

or on landlocked islands surrounded
 by lava flows where a crimson
  and black *'apapane* seeks

the carmine clusters that remind us
 of the bottlebrush trees back home
  our hummingbirds love.

At the sugar plantation manager's
 house we read about a betrayal
  where it had taken place.

Passing over the colony where lepers
 had once been exiled, we follow
  unknowingly in the saga's

footsteps, our own journey strangely
 dovetailing Merwin's poem.
  The last day, after

negotiating a knife-sharp, unstable lava
 shelf to see molten flames drip
  into the sea, hissing,

clouds of steam rising from glowing rock,
 we stop at a church unaware
  that the priest who gave

    his life caring for lepers is buried there.
        The chapel was recently cut off
            by lava flows, an island

    now itself. We will never go back to Hawai'i.
        Neither of us can bear to look at
            pictures of us there, happy

    as we seemed to be. As we were. The tenth
        anniversary of your survival looms.
            Where will we go for that?

    We keep watch for what we didn't know
        then, hoping we don't miss telltale
            signs. Praying there are none.

To a Midge

Desert dusk. The shadow cast by the horizon
crawls up the tree trunks. Moving with it, now
clustered at the top of the sycamores, a good
dozen plump birds, breasts rosy in last light.

Despite the red, not robins. A tufted crest;
the dark masked eye; and when they dart,
no, float out and back, a flash of gold, brilliant
as any illuminated manuscript, each wing tip

dipped in crimson. Damp seeps through the soles
of my sneakers; tiny insects alight wherever
flesh is exposed. If one drop of my blood
fuels this fabulous vision, here, take these

succulent knuckles, my earlobes and throat;
drink that you may rise up to be in turn
eaten by the waxwings, in whose flight
my own spirits, so long earthbound, soar.

NOTES

"Blues, For Bill" (Page 2): This homage to the late William Matthews was inspired by the poem "Mood Indigo" in his collection, *Blues If You Want*.

"*The SECOND Anniversary*" (Page 5): Many of Emily Dickinson's poems reference the Civil War, albeit obliquely. The line quoted is from Number 996 in the Franklin Edition, "I heard, as if I had no Ear."

"August 6th" (Page 6): Manzanar was the name of a Japanese internment camp built by the US government near Mt. Whitney, California in 1942. The land had been fertile with apple and pear orchards until 1913, when the City of Los Angeles purchased the water rights to the nearby Owens River, turning Manzanar into arid high desert by 1926. The internment camp for Jews in Southwest France referred to here was in Gurs. After the defeat of Germany, it was repurposed to imprison captured Nazi soldiers, who were eventually repatriated. The concentration camp outside Weimar is Buchenwald.

"Later, Venus" (Page 11): This poem is dedicated to the memory of the poet Collette Inez, who, together with her husband Saul Stadtmauer, was a serious amateur stargazer.

"Getting Out the Vote" (Page 18): The Rogier van der Weyden painting is his "The Descent from the Cross," which hangs in the Museo del Prado, Madrid. This poem is for Margaret-Anne Smith.

"September Song" (Page 22): This poem is for Carol V. Davis.

"O, Chanticleer" (Page 23): On November 13, 2015 several sites in Paris were attacked by terrorists, including the Bataclan, a popular theater and performance venue in the 11th arrondissement.

"In the Desert" (Page 27): This poem is dedicated to the memory of the poet Marcia Lipson.

Additional Acknowledgments

"In the Desert" won the James Dickey Prize from *Five Points*.

"Blues, For Bill" also appeared in the anthologies *Blues for Bill: A Tribute to William Matthews* (University of Akron Press, 2005) and *Entering the Real World: VCCA Poets on Mt. San Angelo* (Wavertree Press, 2011).

I wish to thank the Corporation of Yaddo, the Macdowell Colony, the Ragdale Foundation, and the Virginia Center for the Creative Arts, especially Le Moulin à Nef in Auvillar, France, for residencies which enabled me to complete many of these poems.

Special thanks to the poet Carol V. Davis, whose friendship sustains and stimulates me; to Lauren Del Santoro França, who captured me in pixels; to the artist Linda Slocum, for providing "Early Bird," the perfect cover for this collection; and to Scott Hightower, Cynthia Hogue, and Alan Michael Parker, for their generous praise. My gratitude to everyone at Finishing Line Press for publishing *Domestic Karma*.

Andrea Carter Brown is the author of two previous collections of poetry: *The Disheveled Bed* (CavanKerry Press) and an award-winning chapbook, *Brook & Rainbow* (*The Sow's Ear Poetry Review*). Her poetry has appeared in *The Gettysburg Review, Ploughshares, Southwest Review, Five Points, Atlanta Review, Crab Orchard Review, Mississippi Review, Beltway Poetry Quarterly,* and *Miramar,* among others. Featured on *Poetry Daily,* her work has also won awards from *The River Oak Review, The MacGuffin,* and the Poetry Society of America. *American Fraktur,* her latest project, won the 2018 Rochelle Ratner Memorial Award from Marsh Hawk Press.

A former resident of downtown Manhattan who fled her apartment near the World Trade Center on 9/11, her poems about the attack and its aftermath won the James Dickey Prize from *Five Points*, the *River Styx International Poetry Prize,* the *Puddinghouse Press Chapbook Competition,* and are cited in the *Library of Congress Online Research Guide to the Poetry of 9/11.* Featured on *NPR,* her poem "The Old Neighborhood" has been widely anthologized. *Split This Rock* chose her poem "After the Disaster: Fragments" as their *Poem of the Week* for the 10th anniversary of 9/11. She has given workshops, spoken on, and blogged about "The Poetry of Bearing Witness," "History into Verse," "The Legacy of 9/11 in Poetry," "Finding the Perfect Form: Breaking Old Forms and Inventing New Ones," and "The Many Lives of a Poem: How to Know When a Poem is (Finally) Finished."

Born in Paterson, New Jersey, and educated at New York University, Université de Paris, and City College, she lived in New York City until 2004, where she was a founding editor of the poetry journal *Barrow Street.* After moving to the West Coast, she was Managing Editor on *The Emily Dickinson Journal* and taught creative writing at Pomona College. For six years she served on the Fellows Council of VCCA, the last three as Chair. Since 2017, she has been Series Editor of The Washington Prize, the longest-running poetry book imprint of The Word Works.

She lives in Los Angeles, California, where she is a backyard citrus farmer. See her blog "On Poetry and Growing Oranges, Tangerines, Lemons, and Limes" at http://fivepoints.gsu.edu/andrea-carter-brown-shares-thoughts/. For more information, visit her website: andreacarterbrown.com.

www.ingramcontent.com/pod-product-compliance
Lightning Source LLC
LaVergne TN
LVHW041553070426
835507LV00011B/1064